Book 2

Coloring Pages For Kids
Animals
Coloring Book

Coloring Books for Kids

By Gala Publication

Published by:

Gala Publication

ISBN-13: 978-1508659419
ISBN-10: 1508659419

©Copyright 2015 – Gala Publication

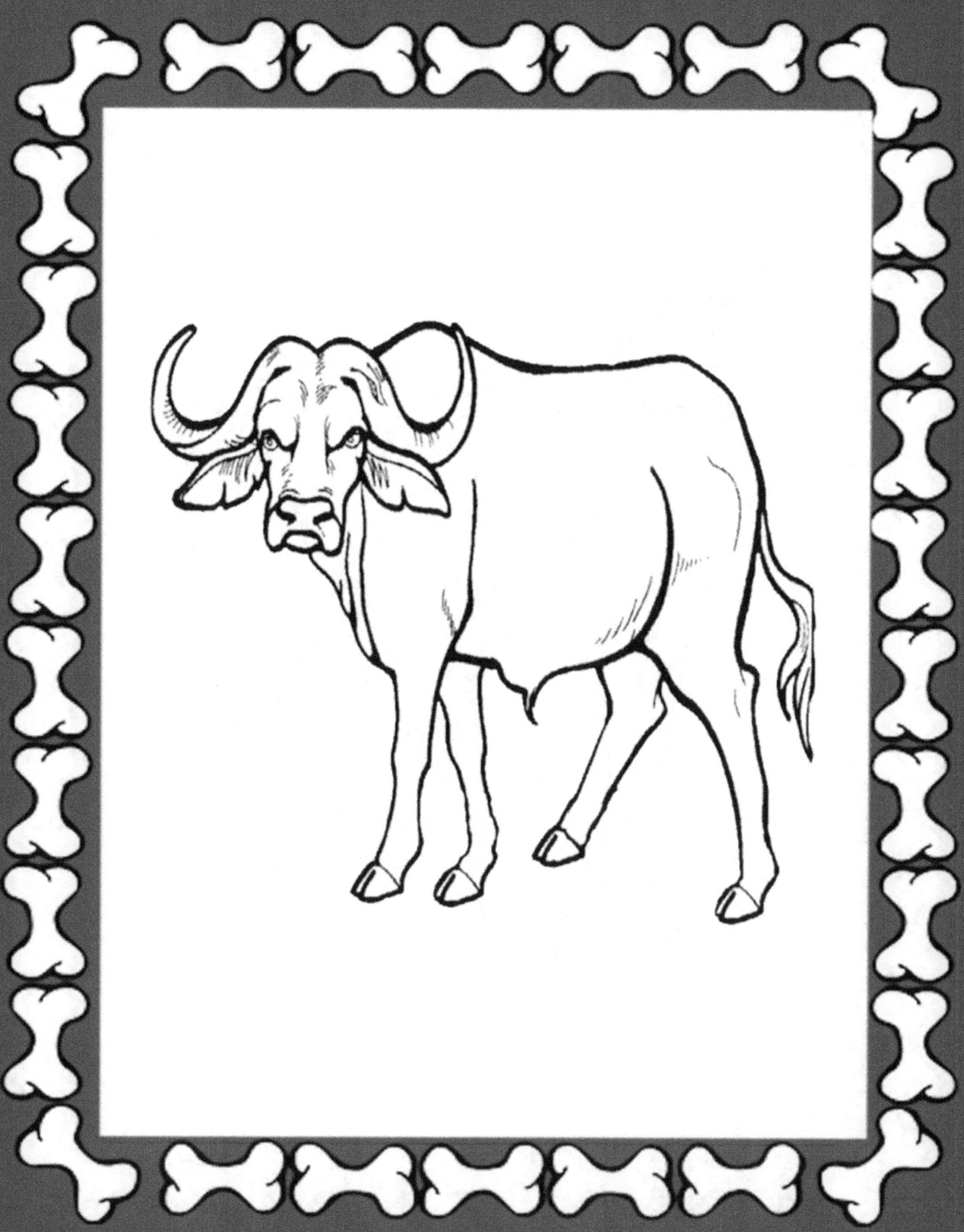

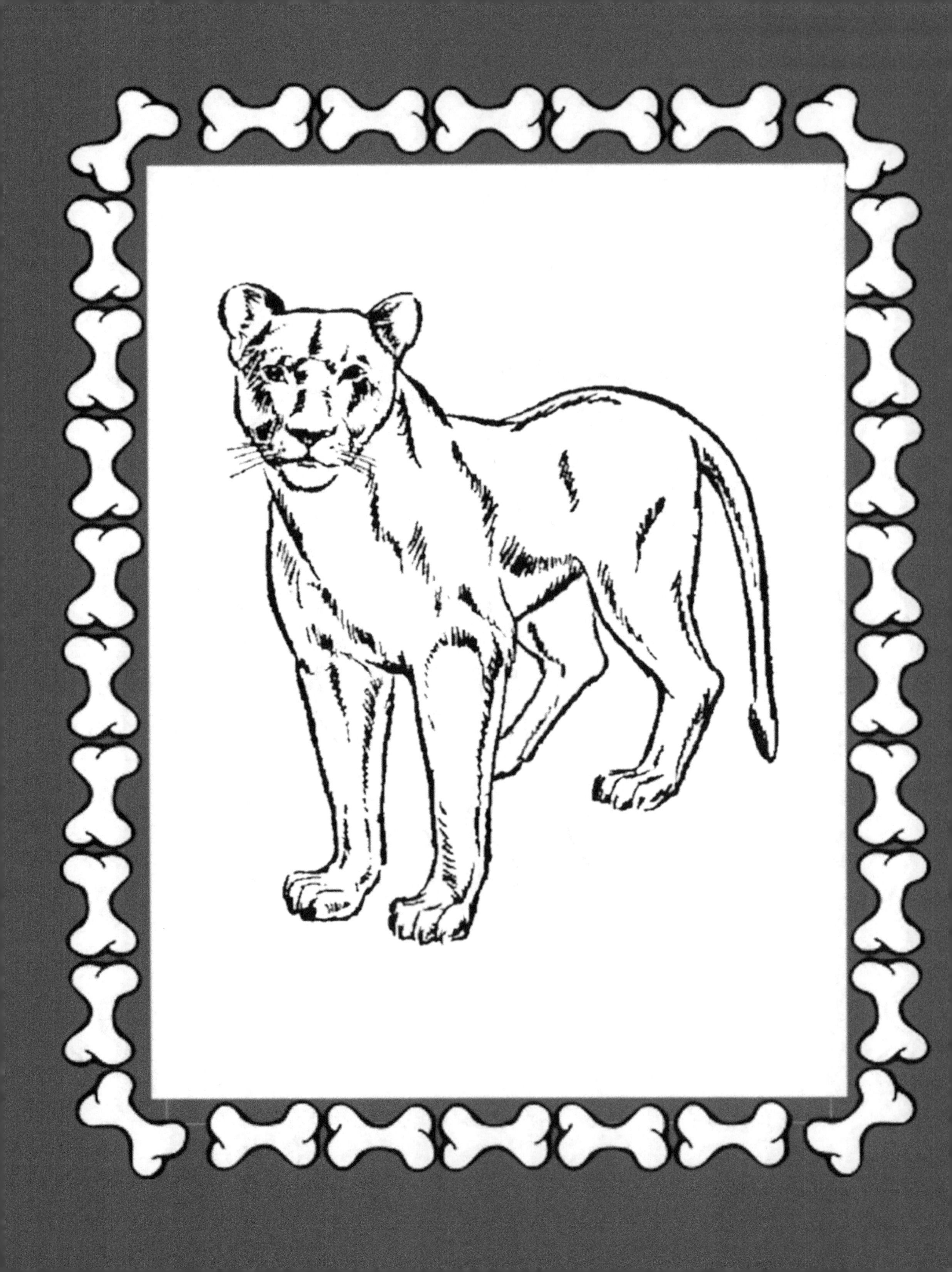

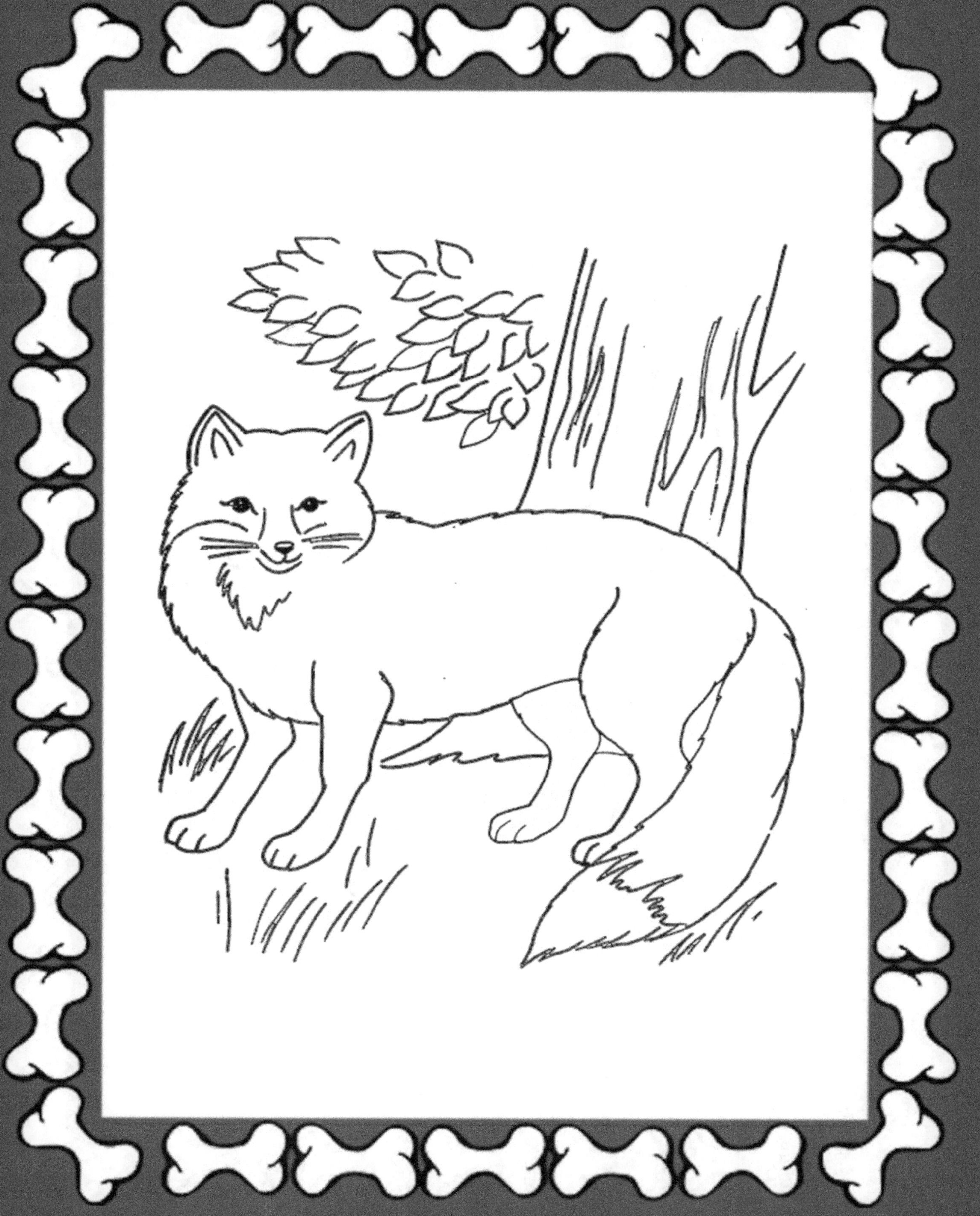

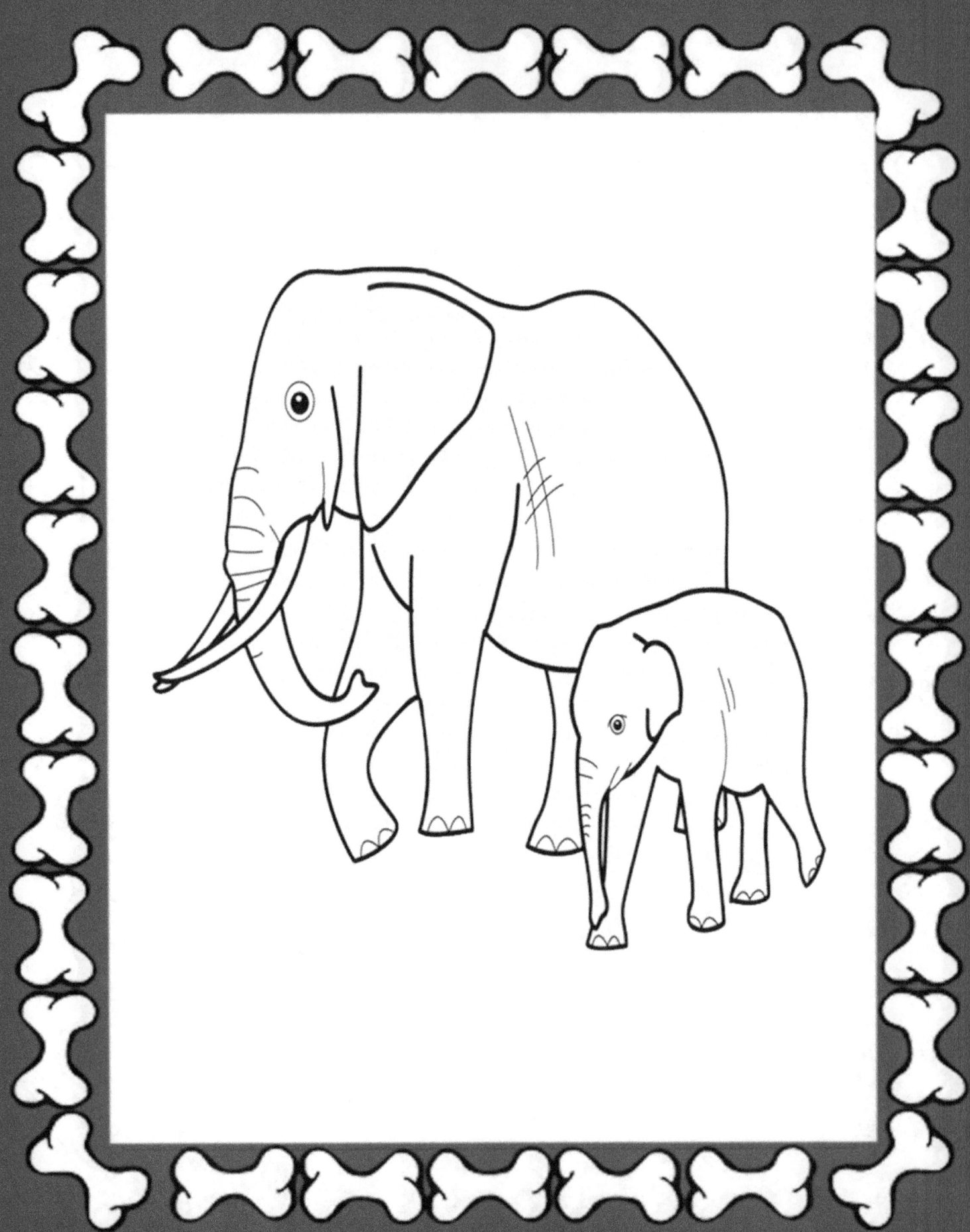

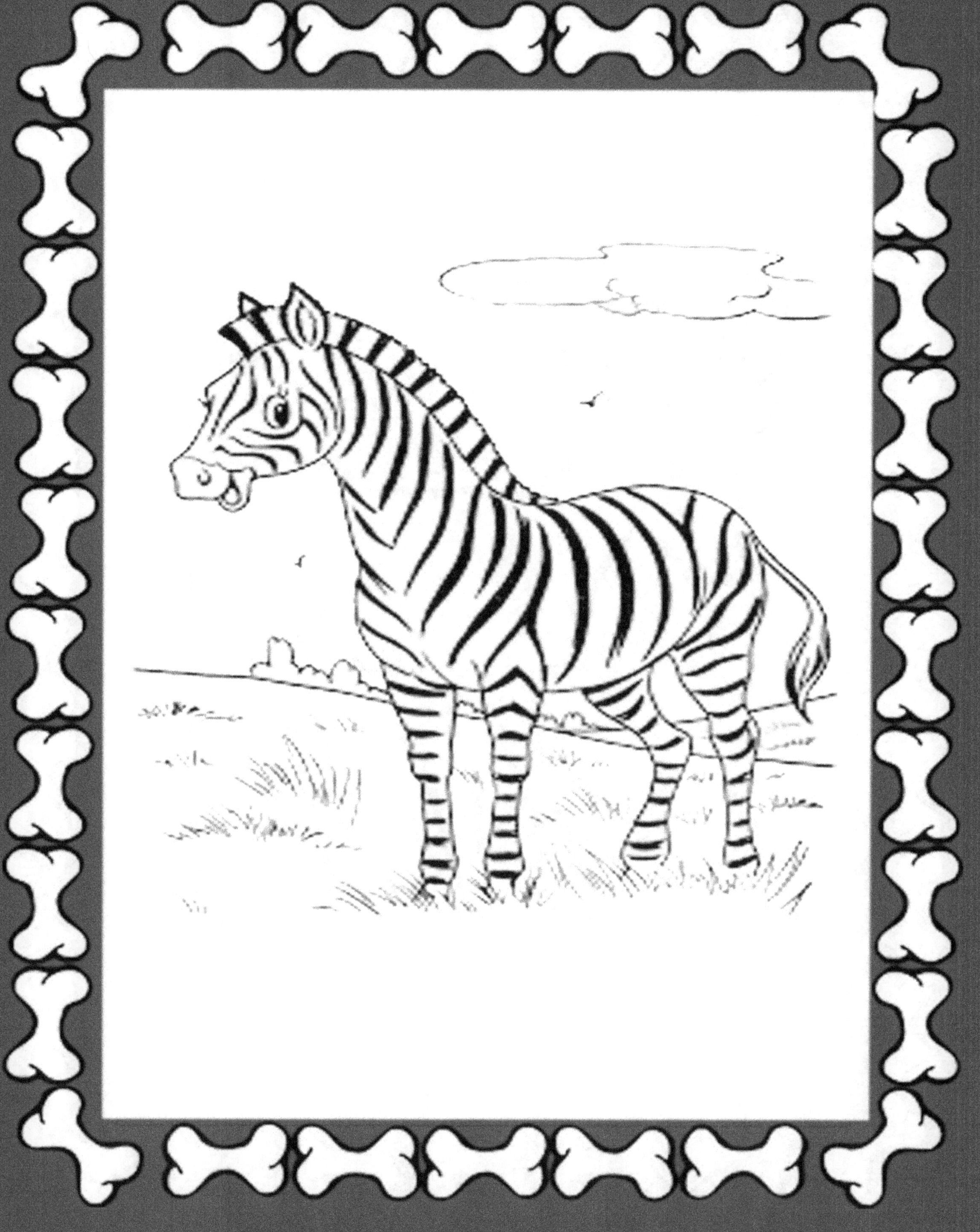

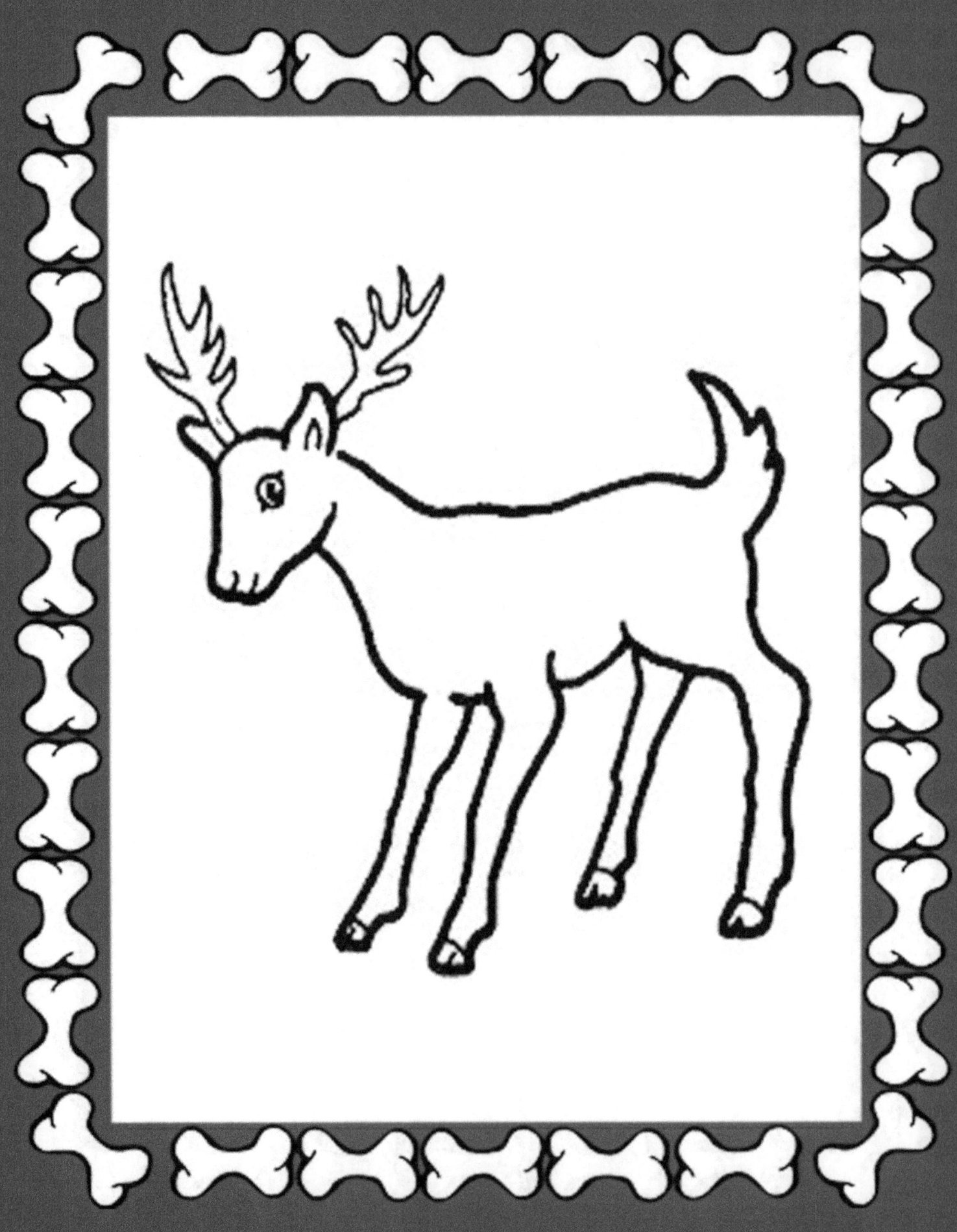

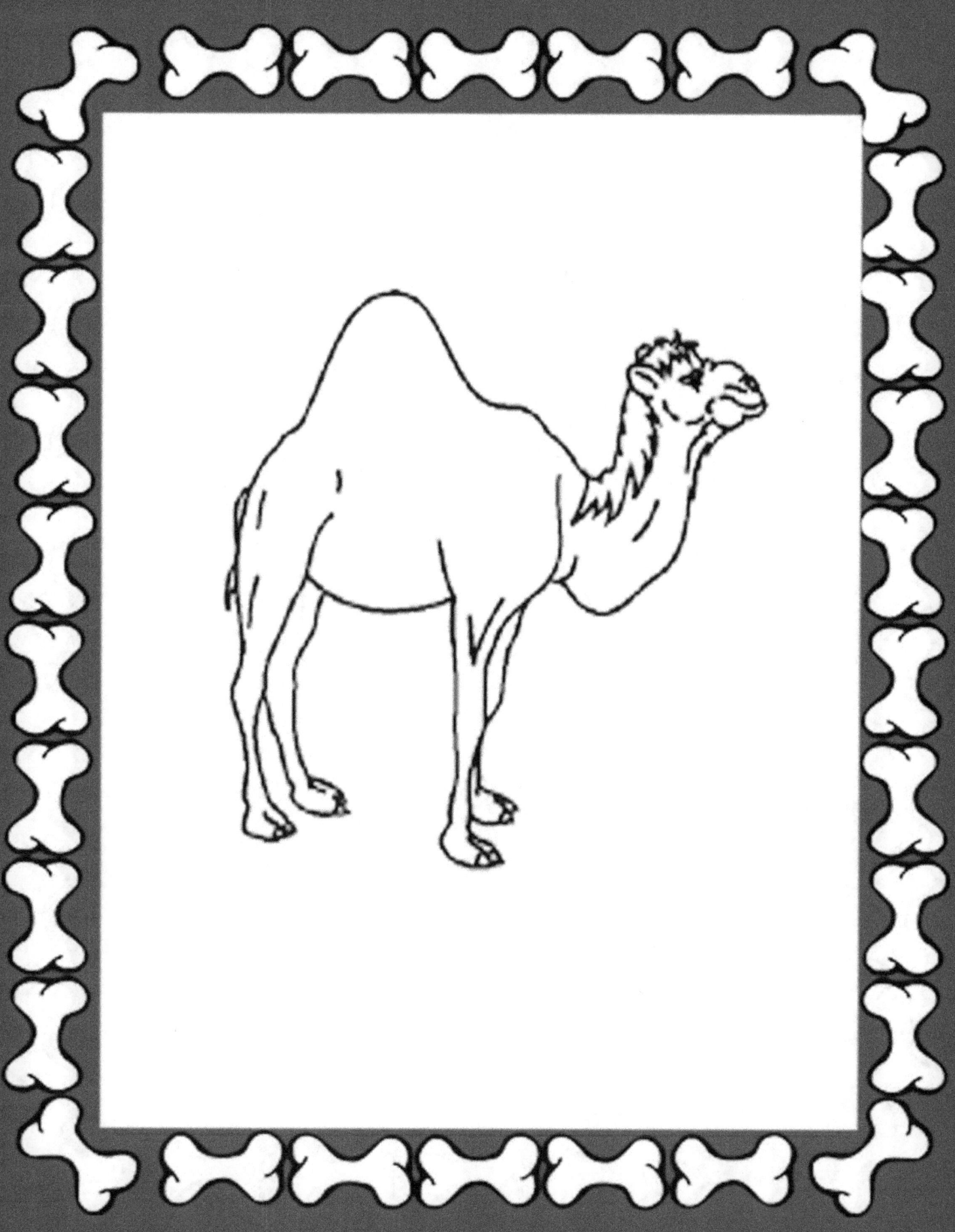

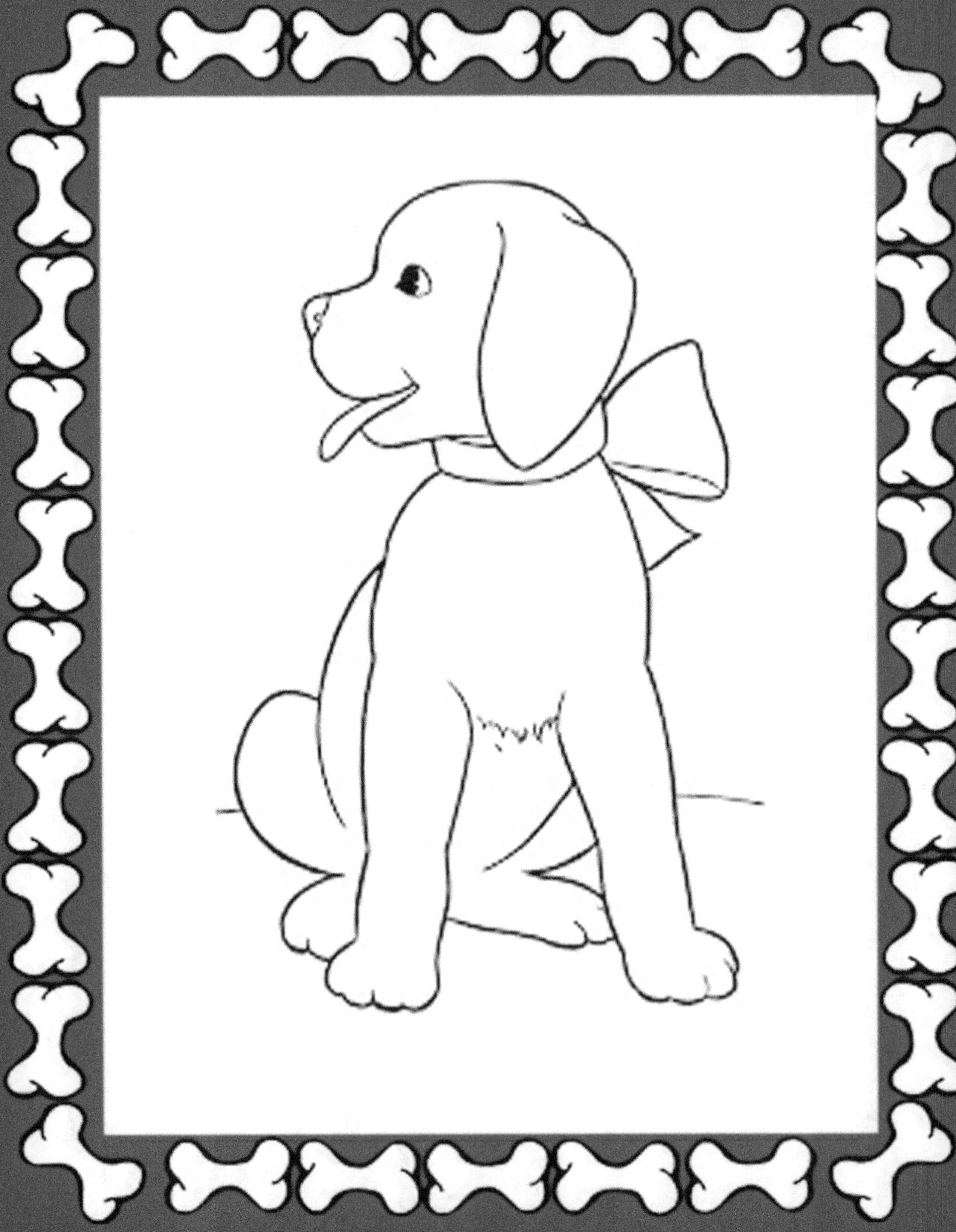

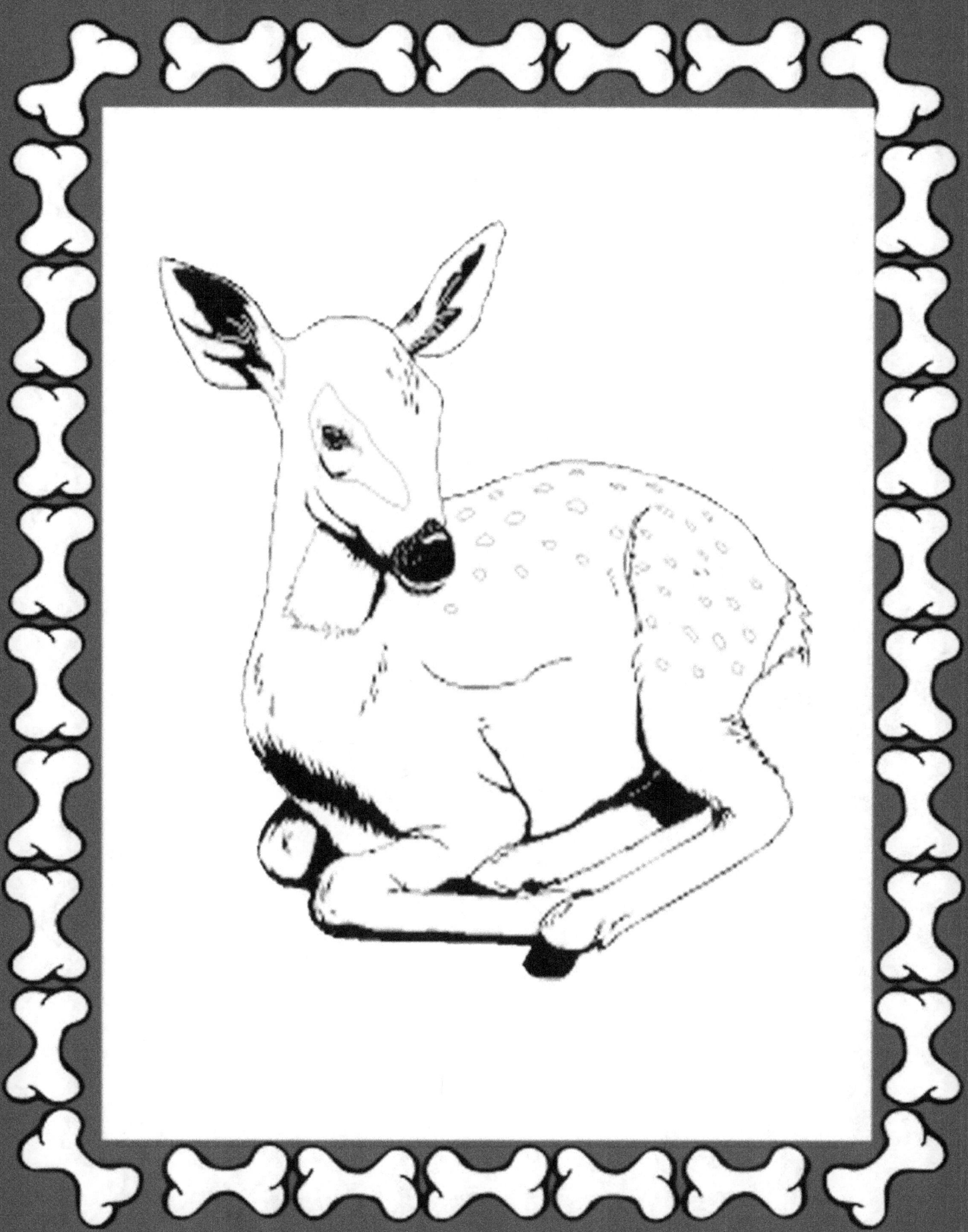

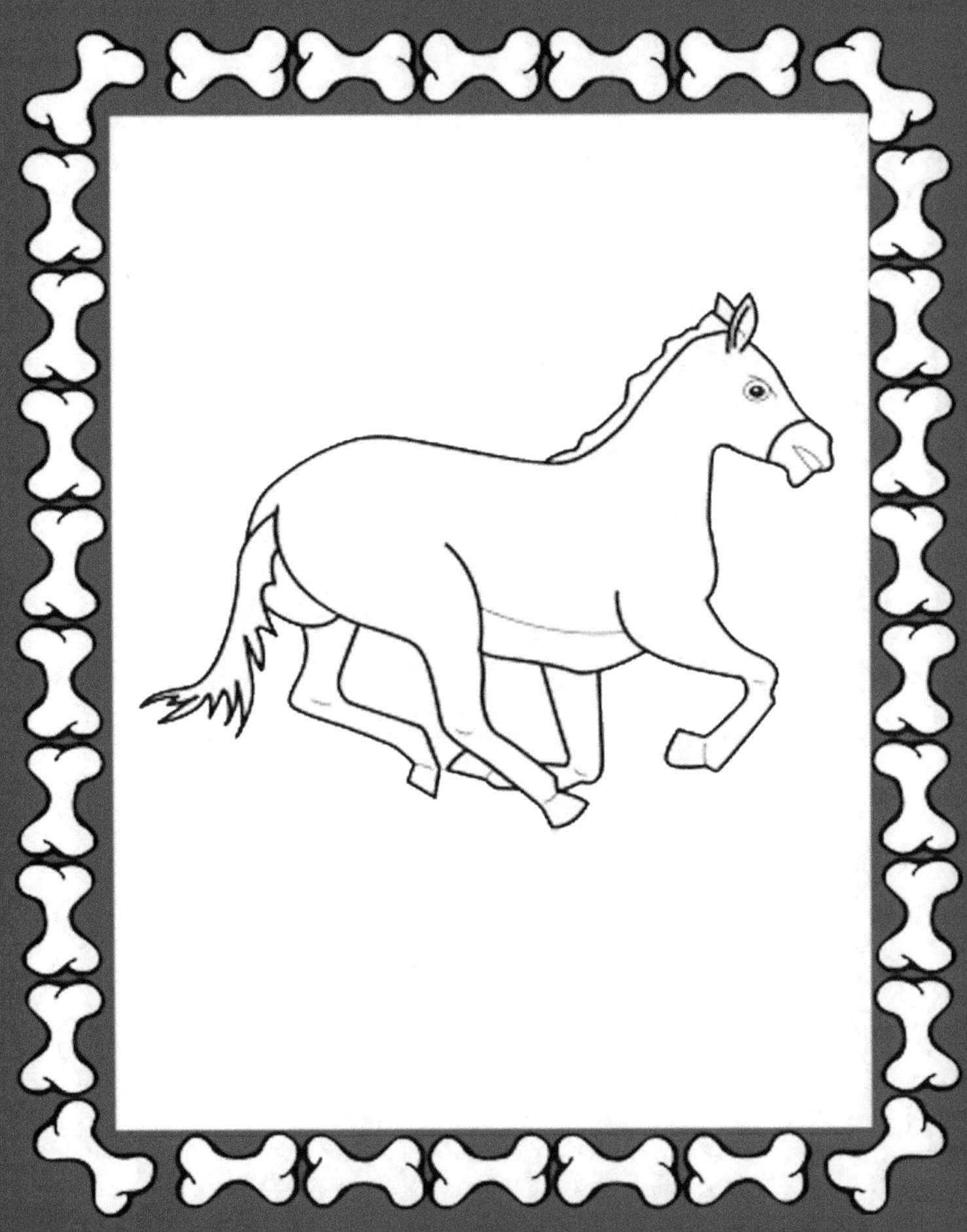

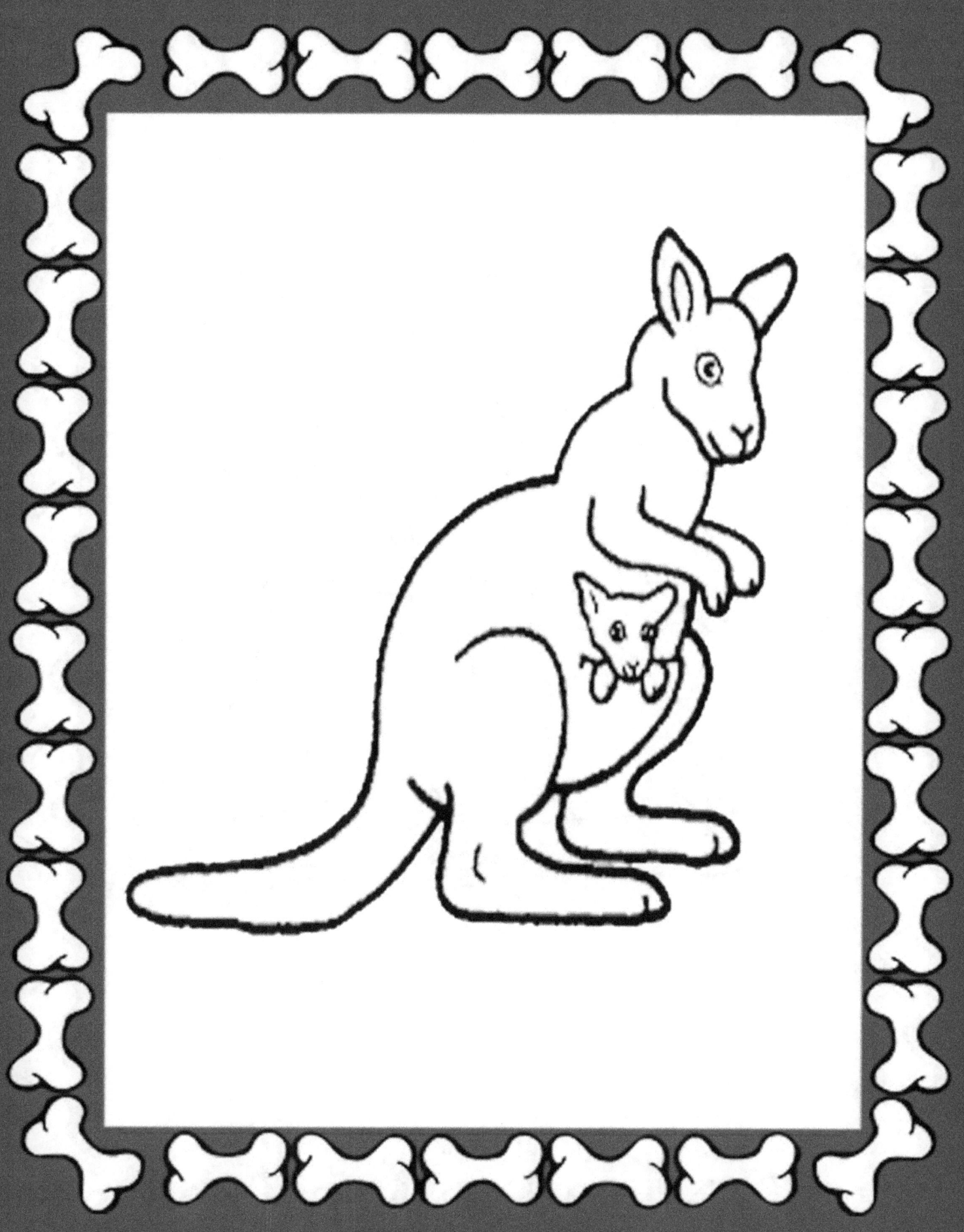

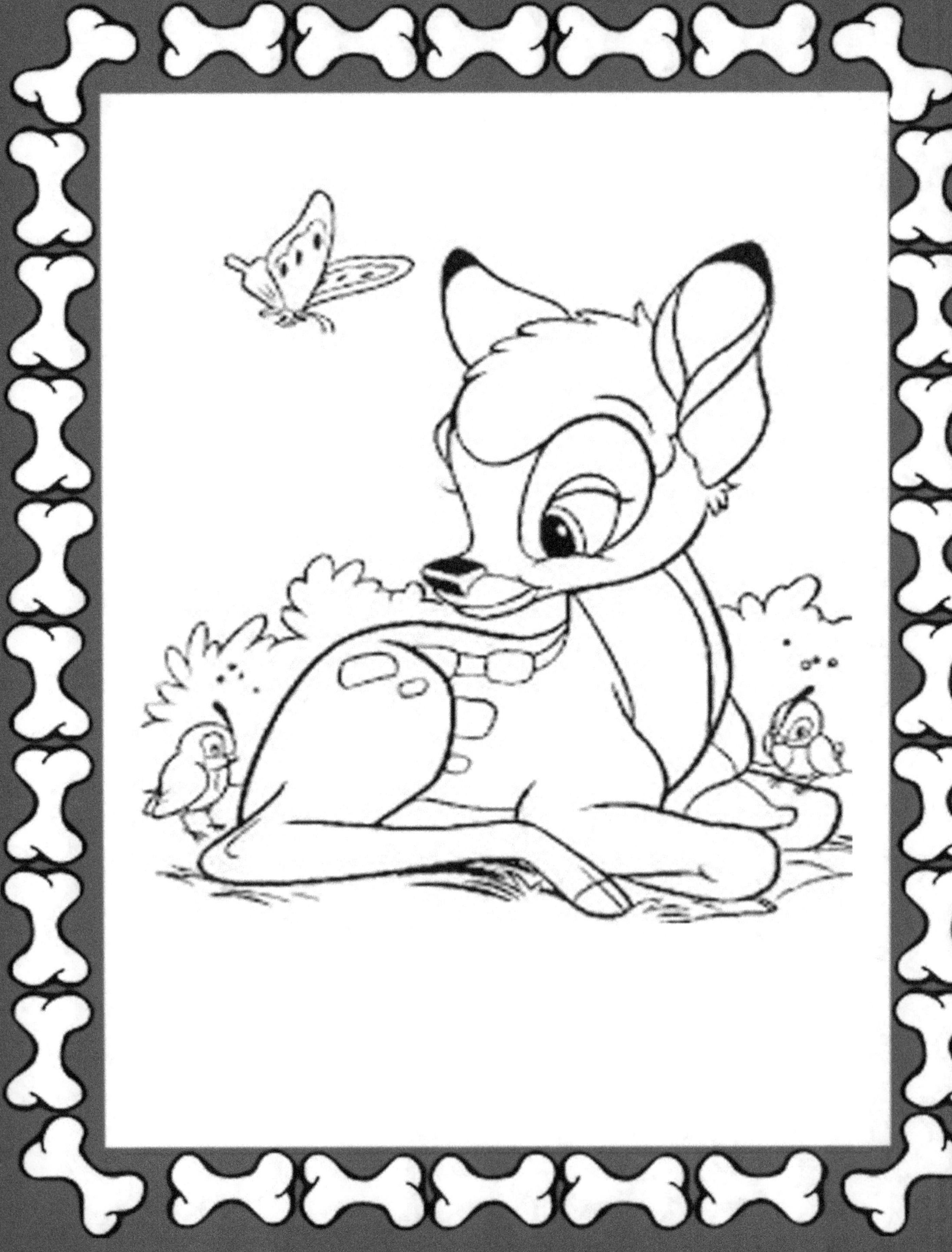

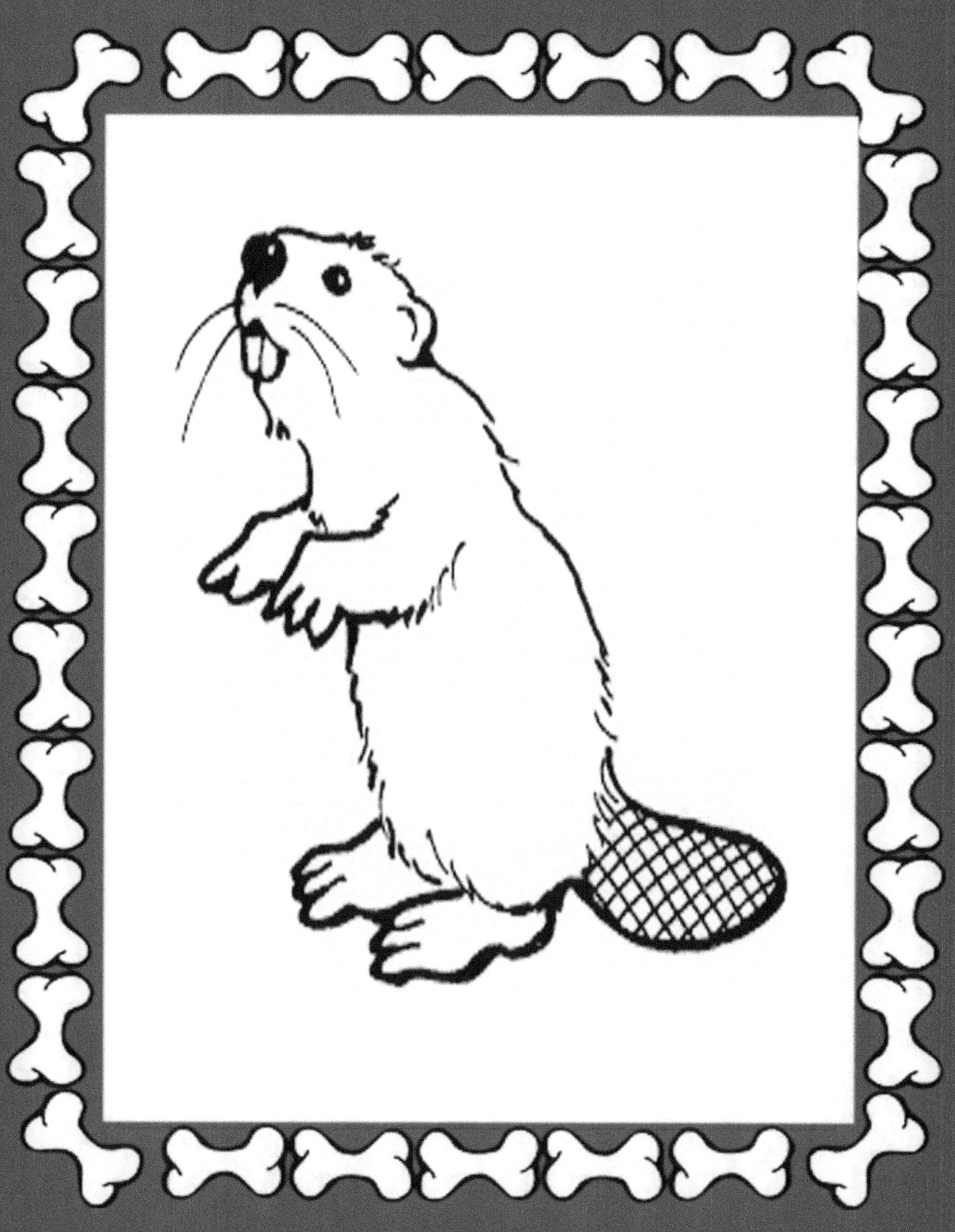

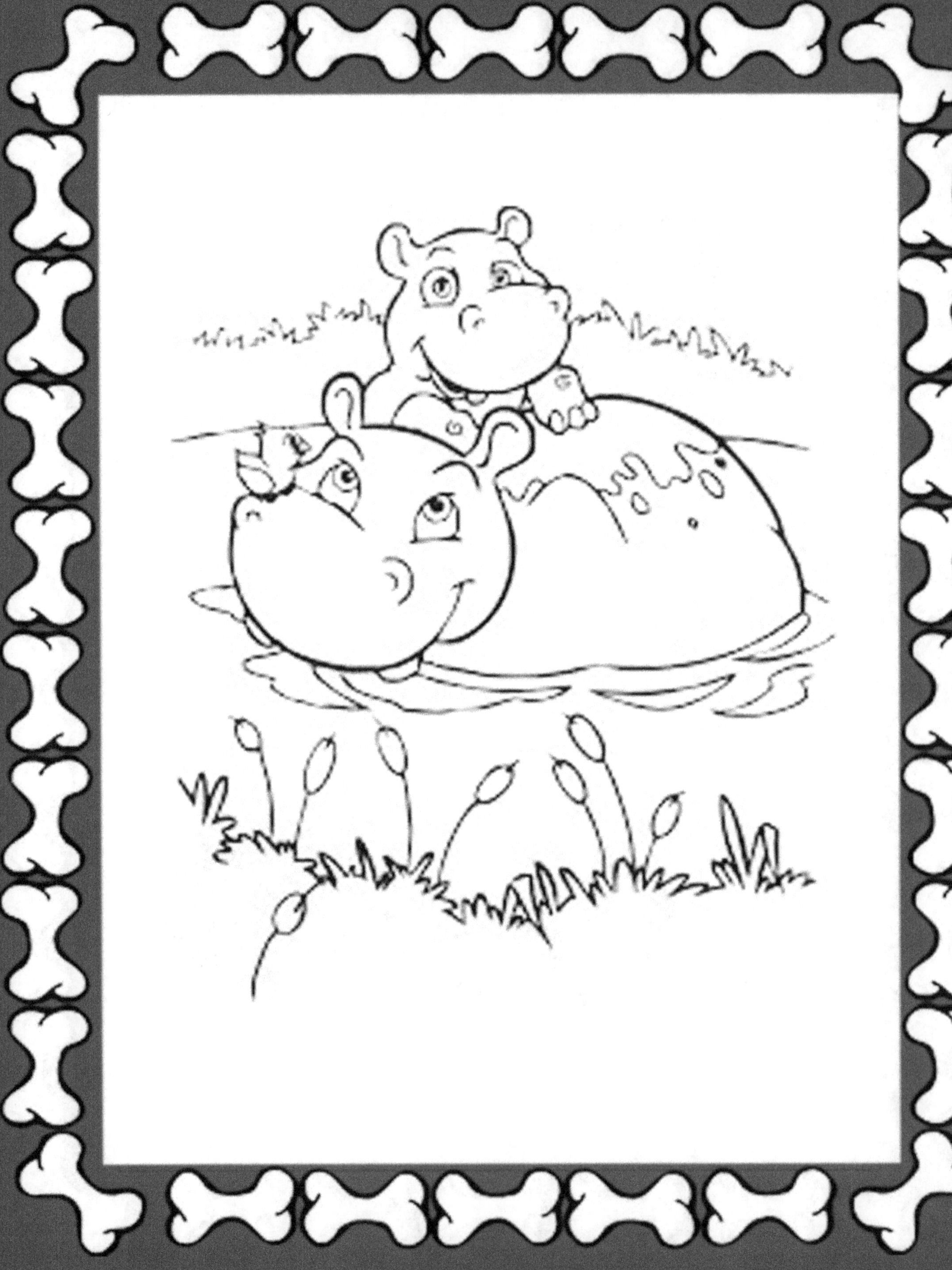

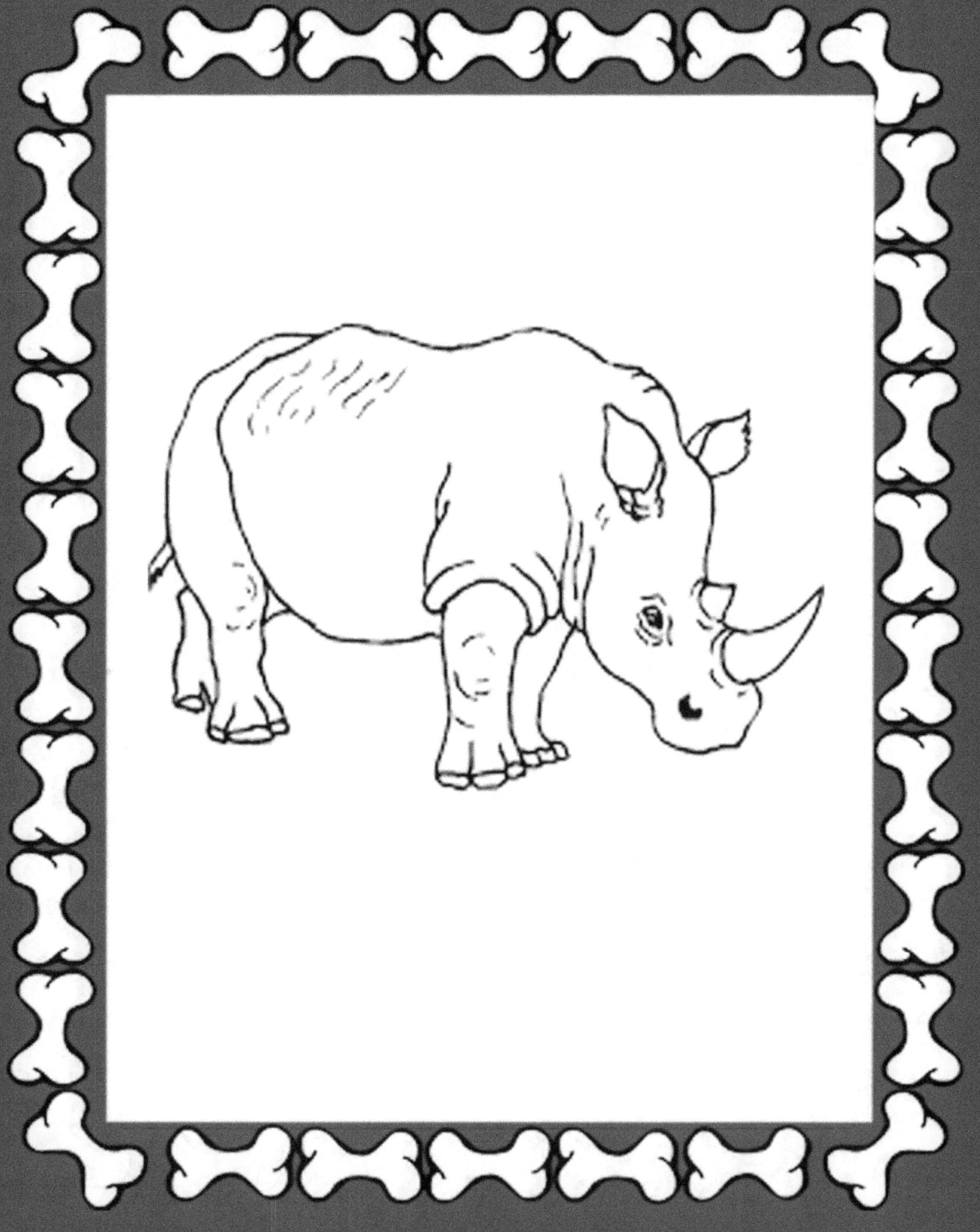

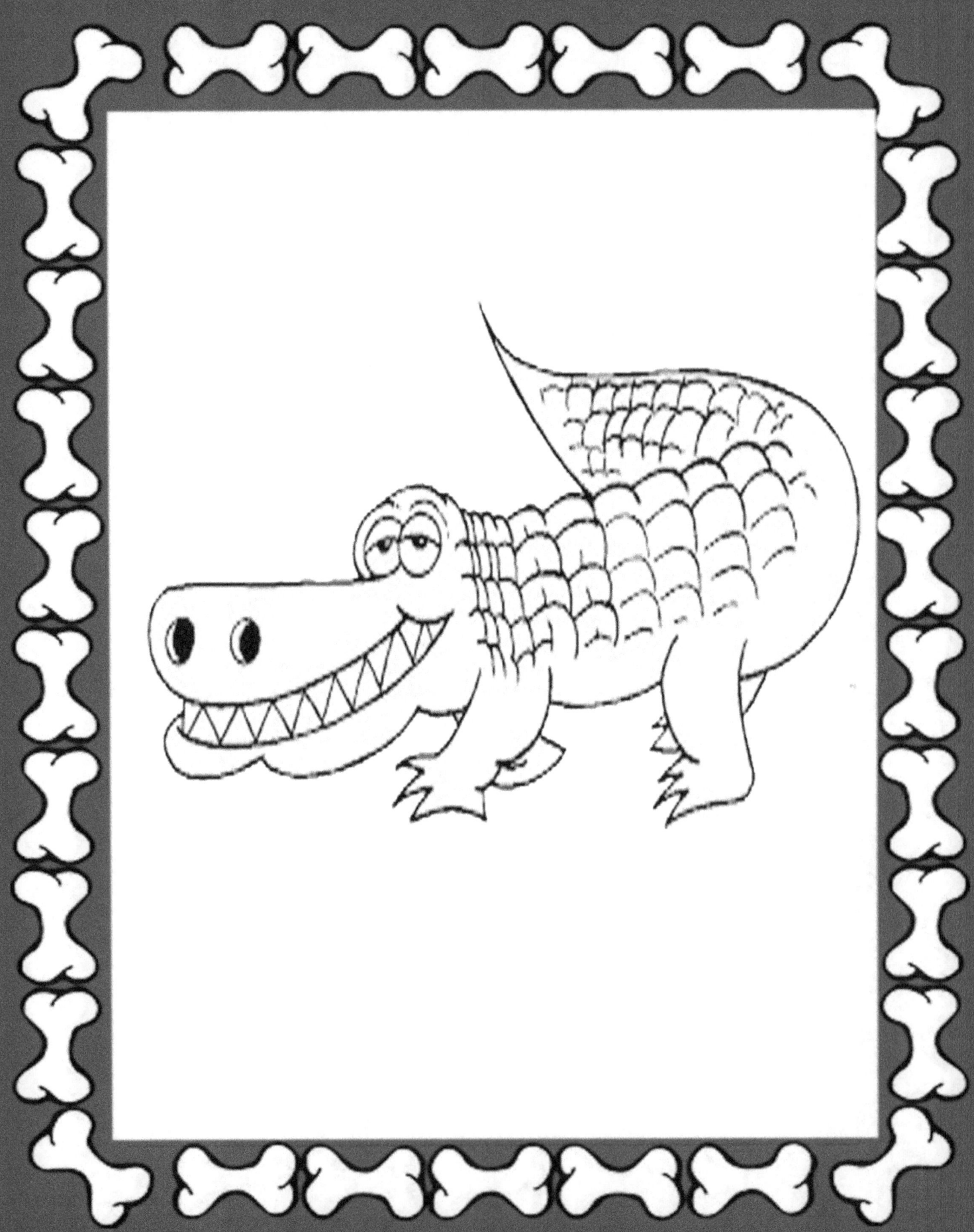

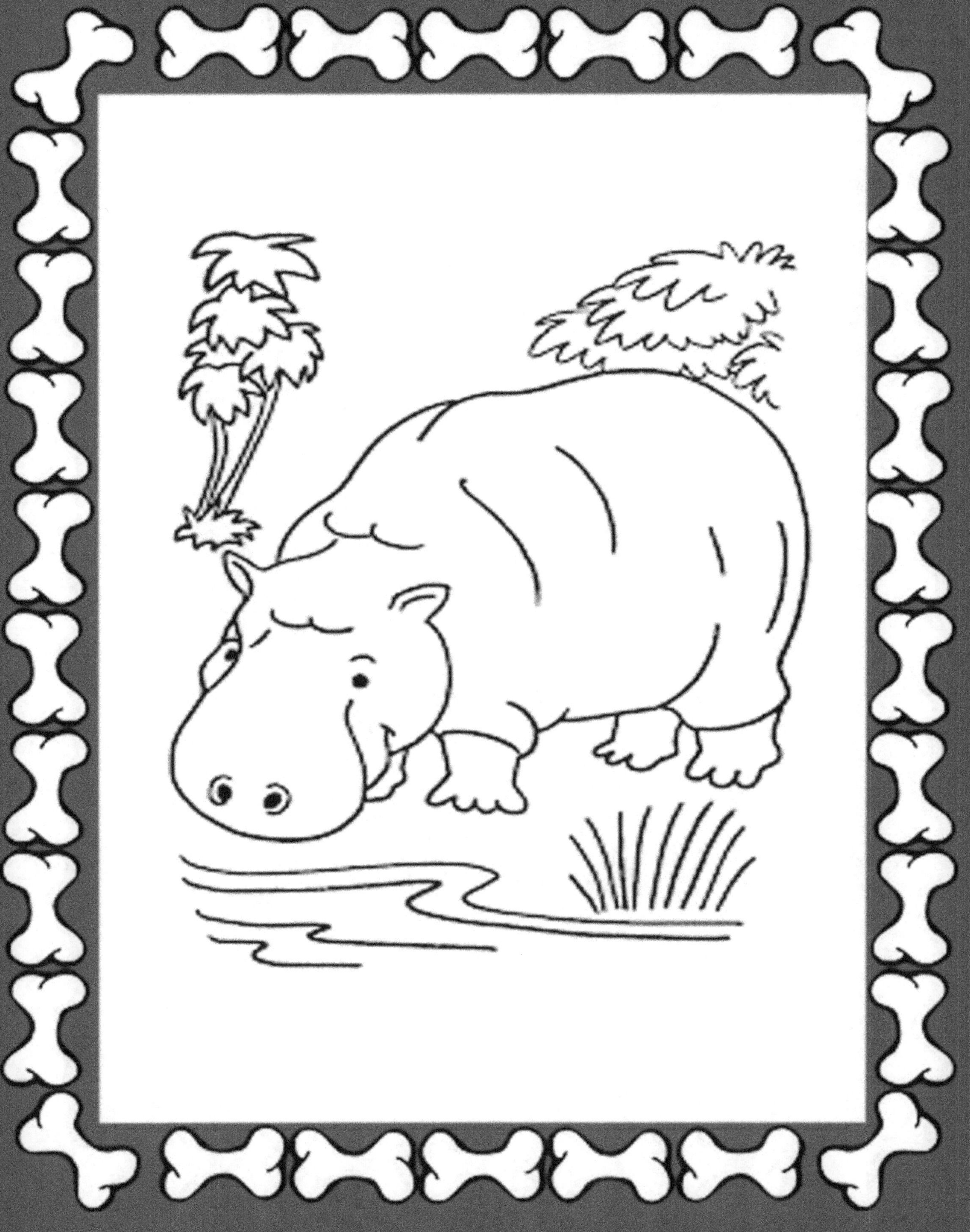

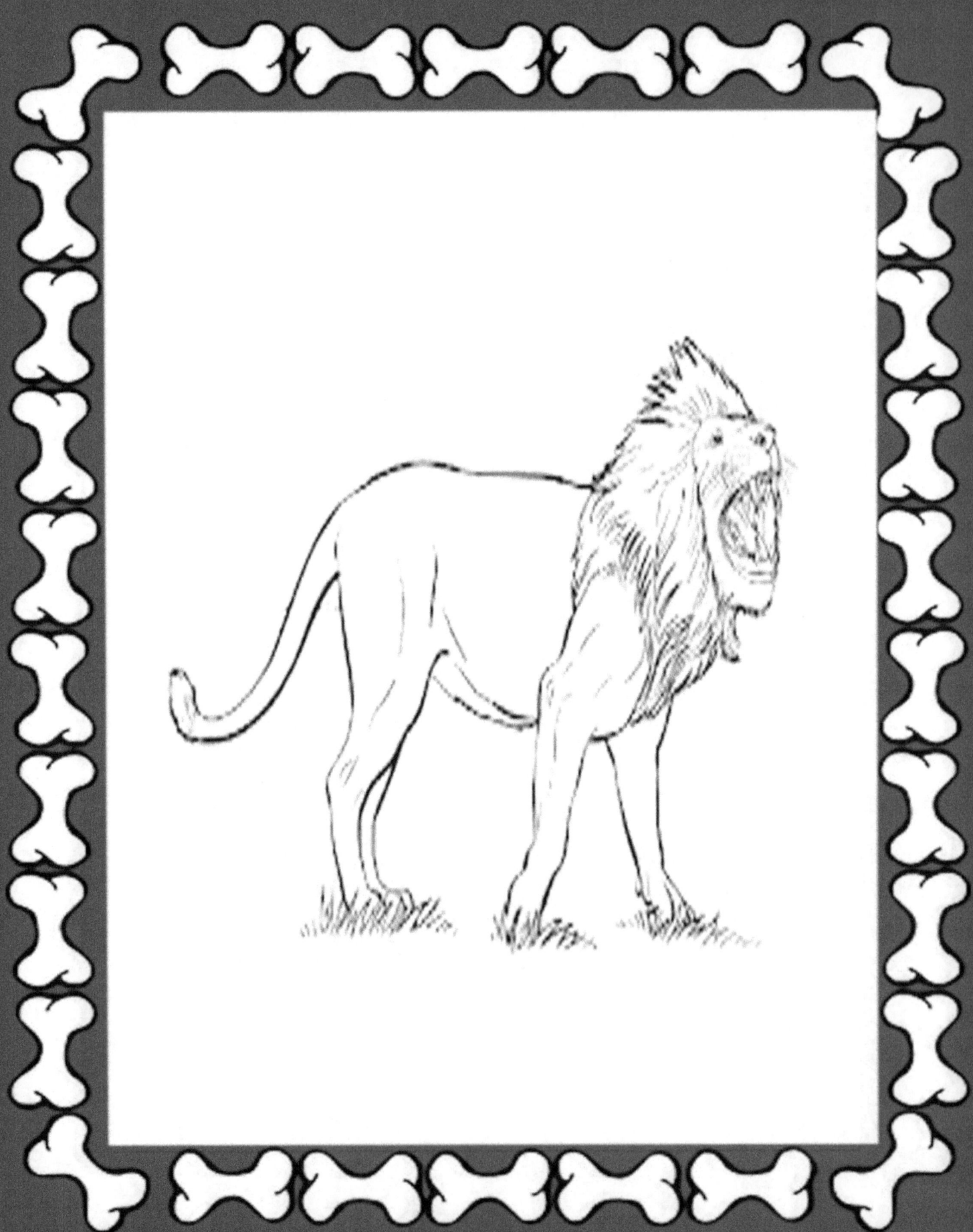

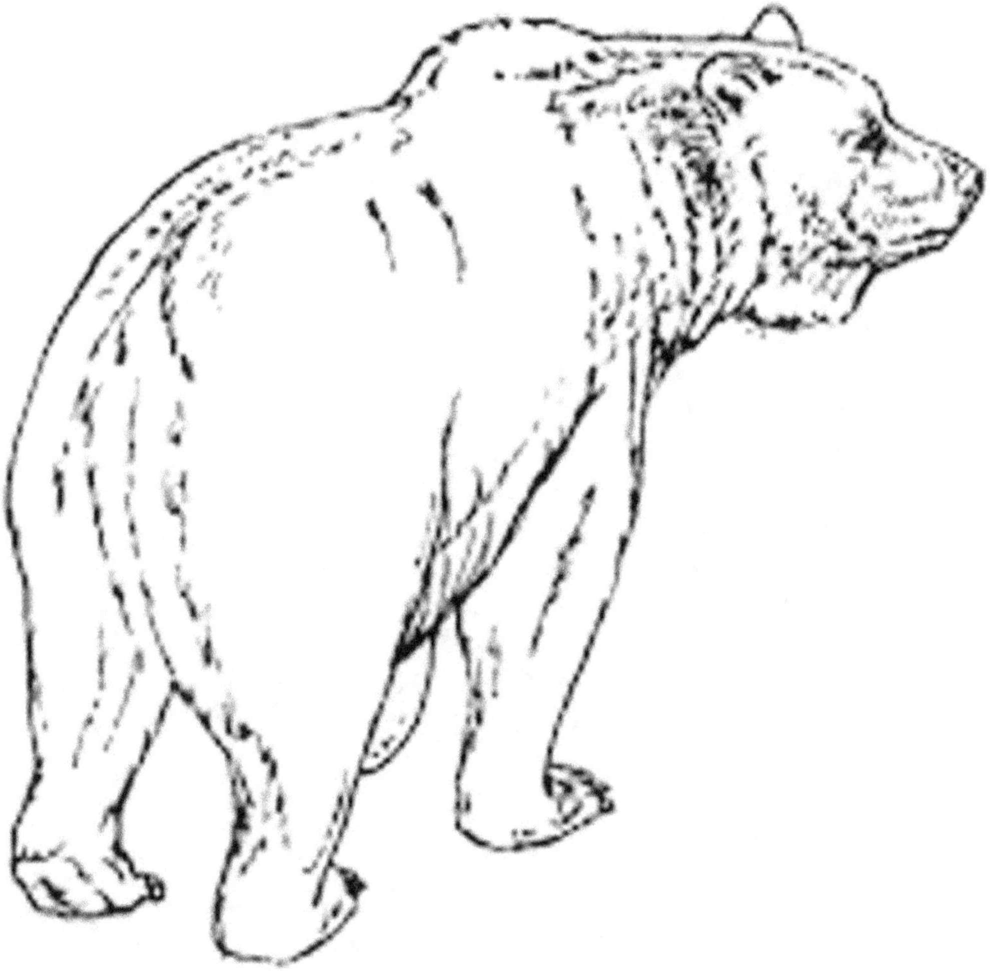

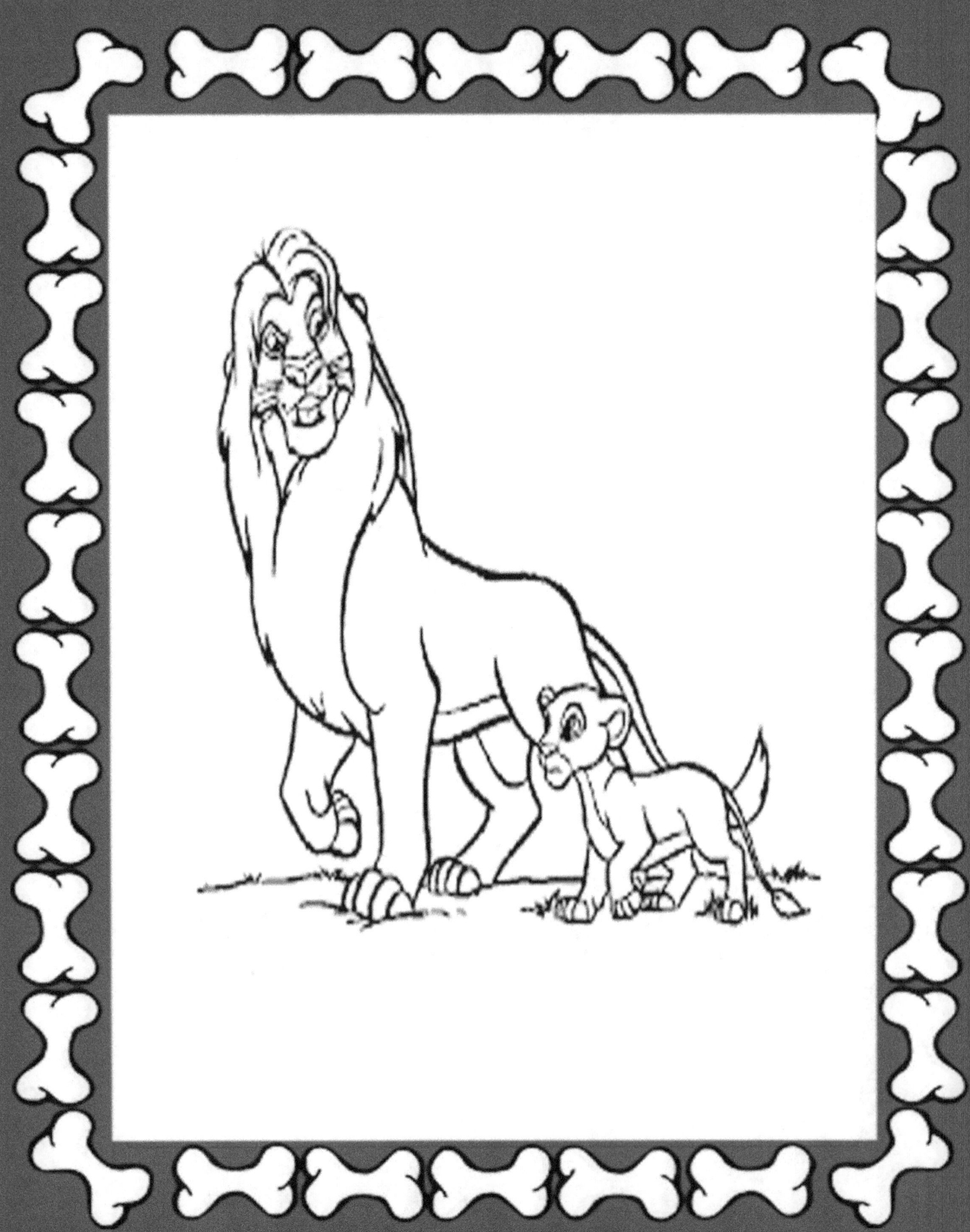

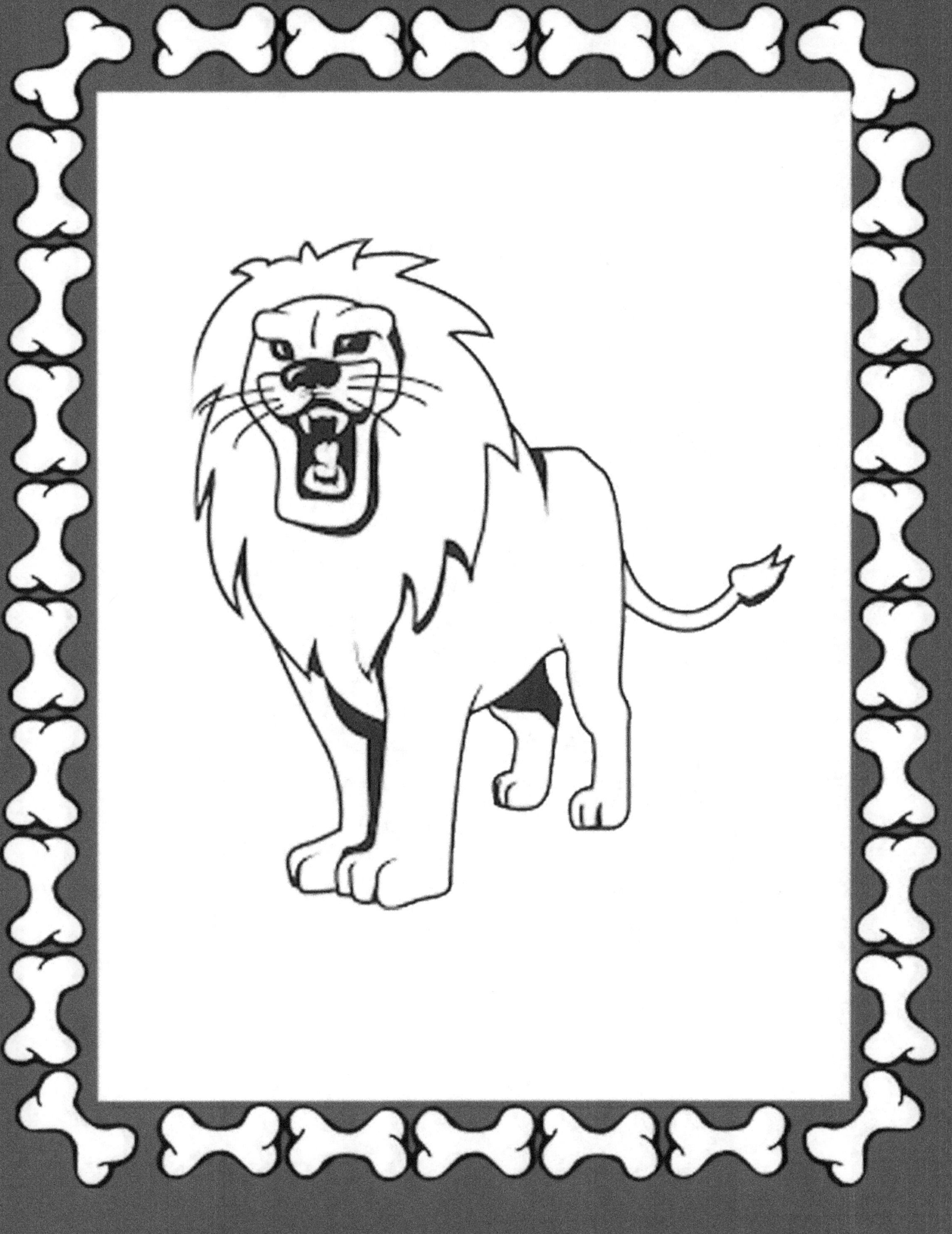

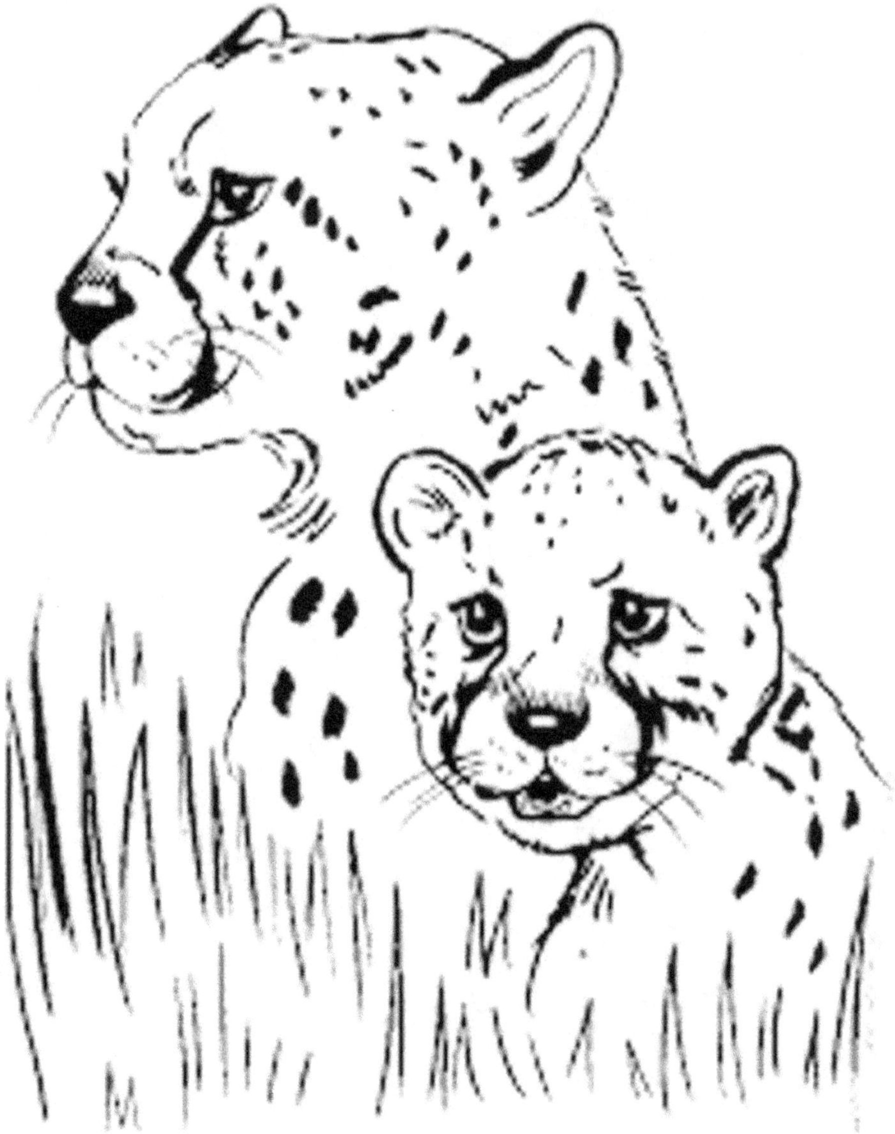

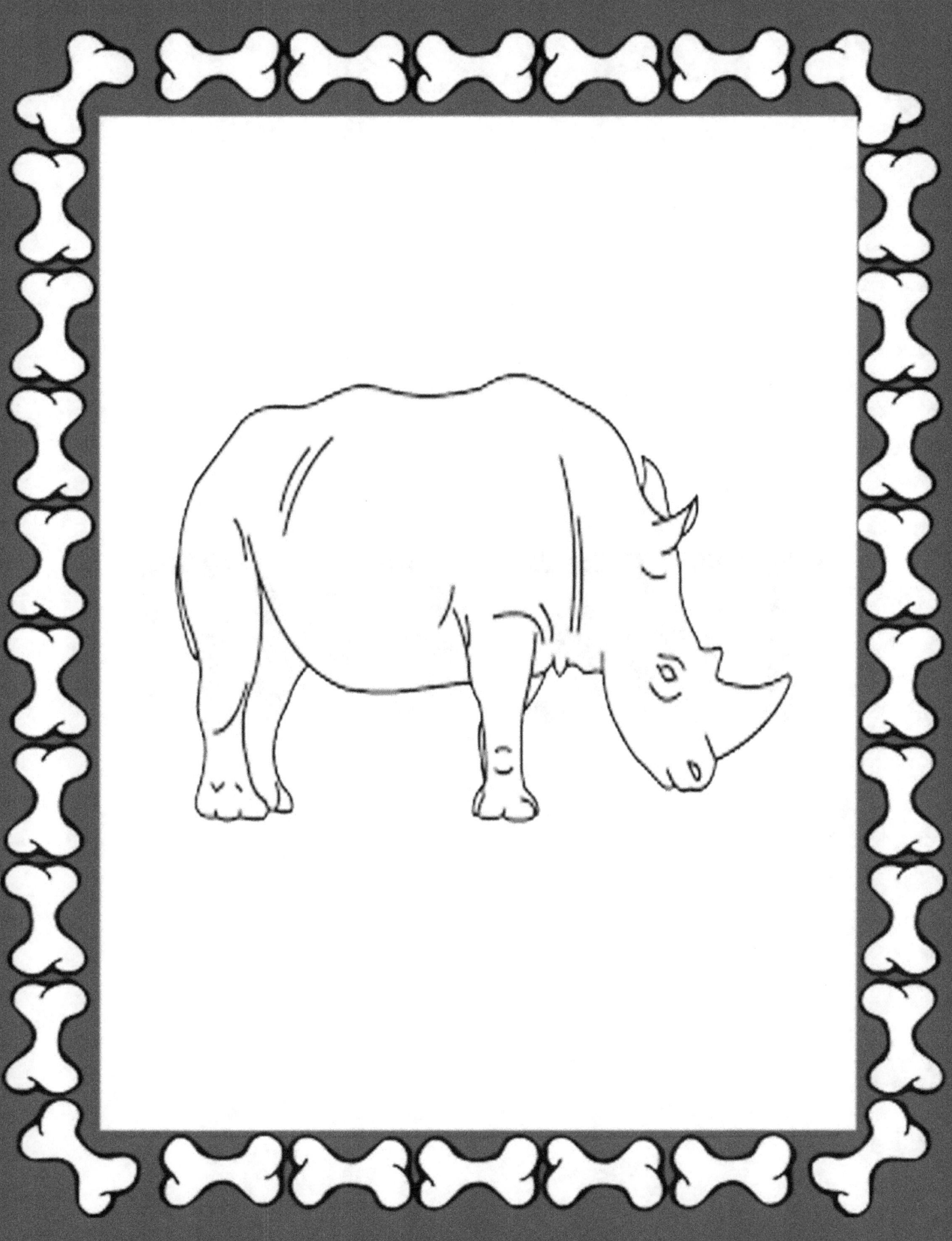

THE END